HARD CHILD

ALSO BY NATALIE SHAPERO

No Object

NATALIE SHAPERO
HARD CHILD

COPPER CANYON PRESS
PORT TOWNSEND, WASHINGTON

Cover art: Photograph by Nathan C. Ward

Copper Canyon Press is in residence at Fort Worden State Park in Port Townsend, Washington, under the auspices of Centrum. Centrum is a gathering place for artists and creative thinkers from around the world, students of all ages and backgrounds, and audiences seeking extraordinary cultural enrichment.

LIBRARY OF CONGRESS CATALOGING-IN-PUBLICATION DATA

Names: Shapero, Natalie, author.
Title: Hard child / Natalie Shapero.
Description: Port Townsed, Washington : Copper Canyon Press, [2017]
Identifiers: LCCN 2016051654 | ISBN 9781556595097 (softcover)
Subjects: | BISAC: POETRY / American / General.
Classification: LCC PS3619.H35575 A6 2017 | DDC 811/.6—dc23
LC record available at https://lccn.loc.gov/2016051654

Copper Canyon Press
Post Office Box 271
Port Townsend, Washington 98368
www.coppercanyonpress.org

ACKNOWLEDGMENTS

The Awl: "Studio"

The Country Dog Review: "Open Road"

Diode: "Was This the Face"

February: "Can't Go Anywhere"

Ghost Proposal: "Former Dancer," "Hot Streak"

Gulf Coast: "Hard Child"

The Hopkins Review: "Person's Ocean," "Screens and Storms"

The Journal: "Winter Injury"

jubilat: "On Magic," "The Sky"

Kettle Blue Review: "Ten What," "What Will She Go As?"

The Literary Review: "Beauty School," "Monster"

Mantis: "Low Blow"

Matter: "Direct Address"

Montreal International Poetry Prize Online: "My Hand and Cold"

The Nation: "Outside Less"

New Republic: "You'd Better Run"

The New Yorker: "Survive Me"

Phantom: "The Mind of Popular Pictures," "Were You Lying Then or Are You Lying Now"

Pinwheel: "Mostly Rasputin," "The Obligatory Making of Amends," "Passing and Violence," "Red"

Ploughshares: "Teacup This"

Poetry: "Not Horses," "You Look Like I Feel"

The Progressive: "Radio Science"

Subtropics: "Absence, That Which Never," "Passion in Public"

Typo: "For Later," "Home Scale," "I Am Not Built for Dead," "Mostly I Don't Want to Have a Son—," "No Radio"

Whiskey Island: "Bath or Escape," "Low Light," "Reformation Window"

for Ruth and Gigi

for Jonathan and Eileen

Memory is like a dog that lies down where it pleases.

— Cees Nooteboom, *Rituals*

TABLE OF CONTENTS

PART 1

PART 2

HARD CHILD

PART 1

My Hand and Cold

Of surgeons putting their knives to erroneous

body parts, stories abound. So can you really blame
my neighbor for how, heading into the operation,
he wrote across his good knee NOT THIS KNEE?

The death of me: I'm never half so bold. *You will
feel*, the doctor said, *my hand and cold*—

and I thought of the pub quiz question: Which three
countries are entirely inside of other countries?
I bought the bound ONE THOUSAND NAMES
FOR BABY, made two lists: one if she's born breathing,

one if not. The second list was longer. So much

that I might call her, if she were never to bear
the name, never turn to it, suffer shaming, mull its
range and implications, blame it, change it, move

away to San Marino, Vatican City, Lesotho.

Hard Child

So I had two lists of names for a girl, so
what. The president's allowed to
have two speeches, in case the hostage
comes home in a bag. The geese
in the metropark don't want
for bread crumbs, despite the signs
proclaiming the land provides them all
they need. I was a hard child, by which
I mean I was callous from the start.
Even now, were I to find myself, after
a grand disease or blast, among the pasty
scattering of survivors, there isn't one
human tradition I would choose to carry
forward. Not marking feast days, not
assembling roadside shrines, not marrying
up, not researching the colloquialism
STATEN ISLAND DIVORCE, not
representing paste pearls as the real
things, not recounting how the advent
of photography altered painting,
soured us on the acrylic portrait, thrust us
toward the abstract, sent us seeking
to capture in oil that which film would
never be wasted on: umbrella stands,
unlovely grates, assorted drains, body casts.
I typically hate discussing the past
and treasure the option, rarer and rarer,
to turn from it, as when K.'s twins
were born and one of them
nearly died—I don't even remember which,
that's how much they got better.

Absence, That Which Never

stops appearing. A seabound creature once believed
to be a single body is actually a thousand small

fish, stuck together and sucking.

You will never hear me disparage this arrangement,
being myself composed in haste and subject to uncoupling.

I, too, am put together to come apart.

A bird screams out my window like an alarm I have
set to notify me when a bird is there.

I cannot say what everyone means

when they emphasize that the faulty ring
on the *Challenger* cost nine hundred dollars only. I never

wanted to be an astronaut, never

asked for any stretch of sky to die in. I'd rather go here,
in the beachhead's gristle or tucked on a tunnel vent.

I just haven't done it yet,

and I know I frustrate God, who built me for endings
and never says anything but YOU HAD ONE JOB.

The Obligatory Making of Amends

Museums of war, they bore me. I'm in my thirties
and so already know every form of human
repugnance—only a child has anything there
to learn. And only a child should come to my play
about heaven, how heaven is given one year
to spend as it pleases, and elects to plummet
down here and live as a man. This means, of course,
a year without open heaven, during which no one,
no matter how desperate, lets himself die. People can
do that, you know—resolve to remain

until such and such date, for a christening or IPO
or whatever their thing is. But my primary fear
about dying is not missing heaven. It is burial
beside a hateful tree. They are out there, yes—
the high oaks whose limbs have offered
themselves for hangings, and I fear that my body
will slough itself down to feed one. This is how
I have spent my whole life. I have served yearlings
to tyrants. I have kept fat each war in this war
museum where only a child could hope to learn.

What Will She Go As?

It was not lost on anyone
that the baby was due to be
born near Halloween:
WHAT WILL SHE GO AS?
We made a list of iconic
infants: Moses in the rushes;
manger Jesus; Baby Jessica,
slipped down a well in '87,
rescued on live TV. Some
people credit the Gulf
War Scud with commencing
the age of cable news, but
it was Baby Jessica, no
contest. Even so, I prefer
the Lindbergh Baby.
Both parents could dress as
Lindbergh: matching
leather jackets and flap hats
with appended glasses,
bomber brown. This costume
works the best if the baby
is nowhere to be found.

On Magic

I have feared God and the push

to explain, by reference to almanacs,
grand moves of the Bible. How recession
of tides and the easterly winds

of the Suez might have conspired
to draw the two halves of the Red Sea, yes,

apart. How the finding of sulfur on stone

in multiple modern excavations
gestures to nothing so much as the torching

of Sodom. I have believed, I have not
believed, I have feared God

would turn out to be like Houdini:
rumored withstanding of any assault, but
in fact it takes only a few well-delivered

blows and a week and He's gone.

Not Horses

What I adore is not horses, with their modern
domestic life span of 25 years. What I adore
is a bug that lives only one day, especially if
it's a terrible day, a day of train derailment or
chemical lake or cop admits to cover-up, a day
when no one thinks of anything else, least of all
that bug. I know how it feels, born as I've been
into these rotting times, as into sin. Everybody's
busy, so distraught they forget to kill me,
and even that won't keep me alive. I share
my home not with horses, but with a little dog
who sees poorly at dusk and menaces stumps,
makes her muscle known to every statue.
I wish she could have a single day of language,
so that I might reassure her *don't be afraid—*
our whole world is dead and so can do you no harm.

You Look Like I Feel

Dirt on my chin and I wonder: Am I already
in the ground? Like a toy turned real, I cannot shed
the sense that I have died. The German word

for heaven's the same

as the German word for sky. On hearing a cruel
prince was in danger, I prayed for him to thrive,
not for his own sake, but for the concubines,

sure to end up buried

along. To my real face, a man once crowed
I RUINED YOU, and though he did, the joke's
on him: he ruined me only for this world,

and this world is not long

for itself. The earth, that ever-loving
but distrustful kin, keeps leaving us just a little
pocket money when it dies, never the land—

Radio Science

Yes I did not believe
the science story on the radio, caught between

traffic and our tornado
test alarm. A blip in utero

can sense the mother's past
brush with horror, from some other coast.

But I did not believe
this finding, until ten weeks in, beneath

the blunt and trainless trestle,
running alone. I startled at some rustle,

and my blood arrested, foamed,
and troubled the dark in which the child formed.

It isn't right. I hardly
think of the past, the gray police and heartless

scorch. I more recall
only the better times at that bar: recoil

of springs in the pinball corner,
pool table that accepted only quarters,

the floor too small and mobbed,
all of us always in range of getting jabbed

by a cue. I more recall
the triumph of dodging one, my back to the wall.

Monster

1.

Eight women in this class, and me the lone

one refusing to say which name I've chosen.
Isn't anyone else convinced of curses?
And regarding being asked to state my greatest

fear about having a baby, it has of course
to do with one of the outfits I have been gifted,
snap-around swaddle all crammed

with dull-colored rabbits, except for one rabbit

that's speeding-ticket red. Why just one?
I would have to be a monster

2.

not to be put in mind of *Schindler's List*,
which is filmed of course in black and white,

except for the one red jacket worn by a child
in the Warsaw Ghetto, then later seen draped
on a pushcart laden with bodies. My greatest fear

is the ongoing nature of history,

its verve and predation and oceanic rage. Or am I
supposed to fixate on something smaller? I recall
with ill feeling the curator, viewing a meager

tribute with disdain: CAN'T CALL YOURSELF A HOLOCAUST
MEMORIAL UNTIL YOU HAVE A TRAIN.

Former Dancer

Regarding heaven, the same fight over
and over. The body rejoins its parts, so what

of the rib? Is it ripped from Eve, and Adam whole
in death? I was posed this question by a former

dancer, injured enduringly from bending
to women. He said WE CANNOT HAVE IT, BOTH, and
screwed like a crowd in which he was trying

to lose me. I remember that country bathroom,
shower curtain printed in "Antique Wall":
wheels and bonneted women and in each corner

the cross-stitch clamor WELCOME HOME.

In those old hotels, I was always afraid
someone would need sudden measures. TO WHOM

DO YOU ADMINISTER CPR? THE LIVING BUT NOT

BREATHING. THE LIVING BUT NOT BREATHING.
Say it thirty times. If you don't break
anything, you're doing it wrong.

Mostly I Don't Want to Have a Son—

too many fears. What if he knows the ancients
believed more boys than girls were born in wartime,
to account for casualties in battle, leave
the world in balance? What if he cannot tell
whether or not it is wartime, whether or not
his purpose is mere replacement? What if he flees
to a field of ice, lucks into a research job
itemizing the stomach contents of terns,
inducing them to spit up their prey for science?
What if he makes a mistake and a bird falls ill,
and to spare pain, he must bludgeon her with a rock?
What if he forges his home on a rockless coast?
What if he has to kill her with his fist?
What if he then finds solace in superstition?
What if he won't breathe when passing a graveyard?
What if he doesn't realize so many are murdered
that graveyards run for miles? What if he goes blue,
endeavoring to avoid the breath of the dead?
What if he does not die but instead is damaged?
What if he must rely on the aid of a dog?
What if he does not care for the dog, and strikes it,
and leaves it out to swelter, and someone yells
I'D HATE TO SEE WHAT YOU WOULD DO TO A CHILD,
and runs off? I don't want to have a son.
A daughter is simpler. All she needs to learn
is neither to speed nor be caught, and if she is caught,
make him follow her to a parking lot,
somewhere bright and unclosing, before she cuts
the engine. Always ask to see a badge.

Old Ad

The English word most warranting removal
from our language is UNBEARABLE;

all I see is people keeping on.

Scrubbing the kitchen, she told me she had three
hearts. One was charged

with delivering blood throughout the dim
aquarium of her body, one was dead
along with her mother, and one persisted
to grieve on behalf of the world.

The Kennedys lost a baby while in office.

I swear to God I hardly think of the past.

Even the old ad doesn't quite make mention
of the great terror we're ordered to remember:

DRINK COCA-COLA. NOW IN OVER THIRTY-FIVE
ALLIED AND NEUTRAL NATIONS.

Passion in Public

Everything now's about Europe, how the tsar
couldn't be killed by firing squad—his diamonds
deflected the bullets. Tonight I'll rent a room,

TV in hutch with one unbudging door.
Tonight, sleep light to watch the left
half of the *Midnight Quiz*. On passion in public,

WHERE IS IT ALLOWED?

fifty percent of respondents say

AT THE MALL

thirty percent of respondents say

AT THE MOVIES

the remaining twenty croon

OH FRANCE OH FRANCE

and of course we're back to Europe, how the leaders
diverted the poison from people's gas stoves,
and the moms all drew their heads out. Who would

want me? I lived with a man who aspired to die
on my watch. I guessed the question: Body or note?
The city conscripted me into its faith. It said

NO ZEALOT LIKE A CONVERT,

forced me to bow to the bridge

O ALTITUDE

forced me to bow to the reservoir

O CHILL

forced my key in the lock

BE A NOTE BE A NOTE

19

Low Light

Young cutting, already with your fronds unfurled
away from the boil of day, weird sassafras,
tell me I am not ill. Some life demands
low light—too much of it, and the great sublime
will call us back. So I lie wan and curled
on the beach of my body, scandal of ocean glass
and seaweed coil for cover. Wetness stands
for sex, I'm told, on film, or is it crime—

snags of hair and gingham on some ridge
and a fisherman calling it in. Tell me again
what I am: dark plant, stranger to pride,
my every joy aligned, as a proper cork,
away from others. Utter unknown men
confide in me their plans for suicide,
which almost always involve the Brooklyn Bridge.
I knew there was a reason I hate New York.

Secret Animal

Seldom one for flatware, I would rather
eat straight from the cup of my palm, as
though I'm my own secret animal: fed
from the far side of a link fence, trusted
in spite of warnings. CRYING, portends
the go-to tract on how to be a mother,
IS A LATE SIGN OF HUNGER. Where
others can, at this far month, distinguish
heel from hand, I recognize nothing.
Just as it is

                    with the dead—we don't
know where they are now stationed, what of
them is disjoined and what remains. We try
to attend to their vehement dimness,
find them in this equipoise and pain.

Person's Ocean

Close enough I have come
to a gull on the beach to glimpse
its pencil-yellow feet, burnished
with black like the rail
in the firehouse. Close enough
I have come to see how

the conch is not my spirit
shell; the conch is truly me, hey
stupid pink turned-in thing thrown
away by the water and bearing
the water's noises. Close
up to a person, you always can

hear the ocean, but it is a person's
ocean: not the lisping of tides,
but the gnash of the boat
wreck, drag of the purse seine,
ping of the black box, muteness
of the oil-undone bird.

The Mind of Popular Pictures

Special sign in the terminal line: NO SNOW
GLOBES THROUGH SECURITY. It's a major
issue these days, all the trying so hard
to bring the city home. Want to hear what

I never believed? In a movie, if a man
gets X-ray vision, he can see a woman naked.
He can see through her hooded coat
and then through her button-down and

then through her bra, and he does not
overshoot. He does not see through her
skin and then through the flatness
of her sternum and then through the acid

in her cells. In the mind of popular pictures,
the body is like this: it won't be breached.
I do like that idea. But I've been harmed.
I know the movies aren't real.

Four Flashes

1. Studio

For safety's sake, the iron escape
folds up from the ground. Bad limb
that won't go down, I'm asking
for it, party clothes the all
of what I own. Even this cat I can't
claim, wandered-in thing clawing the low
tulle in the closet, the dress
my every memory, the cat a flame
in an ash can, batting the fringe
of the window hanging: this is trauma.

Either that, or this is romance.
He lived in an enormous house for artists,
sufficiently dark and malformed
to suggest the interior space of the body,
small peace and the snaps of fever
and light: ALMOST HEAVEN, he said.
I hope to be let in when I almost
die. When you live in a ghost town,
EVERY   HOLE'S AN EYE.

2. Their Winter

LORD OR FATHER, went the misprint
prayer. I don't know which. My failure
to live in Seattle has never silenced me
on the subject of their winter,
dark at 3pm. That city so quick to dim,
seat of the Great Pacific Shame Belt.
On the interview show, a woman
with a head wound, or born that way,
I forget. She claimed the most incredible
memory known ever to man or science,

the roughest part the inability to banish
her hideous youth, bleating not
as radio banned on the transit line, but din
of what legal instrument the voice is.
WE ALL HAVE MADE (she said
this twice)   BAD CHOICES.

3. Direct Address

I'm trying to find out who wrote
every prayer, but it isn't the wisdom
most readily dug up, not like WHEN
TRAINING A DOG YOU MUST LOOK IT
IN THE EYE or other aphorisms
of good sense. Yes, I'm in line to get bit,
never checking, long swearing
that F. Scott Fitzgerald so pitied
newsboys out in the rain, he would buy
all their papers. He was named
for Francis Scott Key, and likely
knew where to give thanks
for that, but not for prayers, of which
there are many, uttered up to the same
God or none, if one's faith forbids

the specific. They say war's no time
to shy from direct address, the foxhole
cry or hideous bomb someone
inscribed   DEAR VIET CONG.

4. Open Road

He said he was never not thinking
of Vietnam—even in the course of acid
trips, he kept himself busy recalling,
the others all napping or shouting
about the Hays Code and how early
movies couldn't show anyone getting
away with a crime. They used every part

of the system, as East Germans are said
to have used every part of the car:
underside of the seats hollowed enough
for a folded man, compartment for infants
pressed from a bassinet mold, I DON'T
KNOW, BUT   I'VE BEEN TOLD.

I Am Not Built for Dead

bodies—my people in their tsarist shanties
wouldn't have come seen one, only attending
funerals for their own. They came to this land
of table wakes and windowed typhoid caskets
so I could have a new life mourning
those whose books permit remembrance in
the open light. America: the old bureau
that fell on me when I opened too many drawers.
Someone approach and remove it, please, but not
you or you or you—yes, now I see
everyone good is gone, for everyone good
I've averted my eyes and sung OH LET THE CIRCLE,
and all remaining compatriots are awful:
despots too old to be tried, artists in want
of adulation, the couple where the woman
has a kind of tic and makes a racy comment
every twenty minutes. She sucked off a stranger,
she told me, during a stay in the French Quarter,
and her husband snapped then in her turtle face:
NOBODY CARES. EVERYONE HAS A PAST.

Seven Wounds in Two People

How Dallas, the name of Dallas, the whole
of Dallas seemed to be tainted after the shooting.

WHAT A BLACK EYE FOR THE CITY. NO ONE
WILL GO THERE.

I thought I could help by remembering Dallas

instead for the soap opera bearing its name,
the sort of story in which people rouse—

defying expectation, after a run of slow seasons—
from biometric stasis, and then are swarmed by experts

asking DO YOU KNOW WHERE YOU ARE? and WHO

IS THE PRESIDENT?

Winter Injury

Burn from a worsted rug that will not display
for a full day, welcome home. All I have coming in this
world is a joke that hits me later. I was ever the hampered
child, doting on what could not feel, unwilling to walk
on stairs that creaked for fear it hurt the house.
I never knew a thing about crying out, when to come running,
when to run. How, as with the lowing of
a simpler species, pain is the body's way of making meaning.
My old love handled me hard and I thought nothing.

Yesterday I happened across a killed cat on the road.
Someone had hit it. It was then I wondered: Could that be me?
Am I that cat, cut down from the world
for hours now, oblivious, seeing myself only
as a witness? I went to touch the body but was afraid,
afraid of my own body and what disease I carry
in death. I remembered meeting a child at a funeral.
She could recite all the times an animal
escaped from a zoo enclosure. I remembered I am no cat,
hardly wild as to require a wall, but instead a bird dog falling
in snow, splaying, pulling up, bearing in
my mouth some little trauma like a pheasant, blood
in the feathers and me, bred never to break the skin.

Again I resolve to move. A woman lists
a near room in a floor-through with piano. I have no use
for any box of hammers, but still I reply, having been raised
as though in a family of weavers, where it falls
on the smallest ones to watch for faults. The young
among us traffic in the ragged, dinner sonatinas
seldom the rage. My old love handled me hard. I let it happen.
The songs I like are mostly swears and clapping.

Screens and Storms

Our garden grew enormous not from care,
but from neglect. I slept there, covered in bells
so I would wake if anything tried to harm me.
Of the two types of windows known, he threw
himself from neither, over and over. A bird
clock, he extended his body past the sill
but never dislodged from the structure, chiming on
about how he couldn't
                              die if he tried.

Who left this lab to me? Viewing a cabbage
by microscope, I proceed with only reverence,
while for my own body, I feel nothing but pity.
It's so naive. It follows me here and there
like a lovesick person, fetching my essentials,
shoeless on the slate floor in the cold or cramped
in a truck for a thousand miles, and yet I don't
even like it. I wouldn't
                              cry if it died.

Bath or Escape

After a bath or escape, the dog
stands newly without his collar
and everyone coos *ohh aww he's
naked*, as though he weren't
on full display before.
This sheer unbrokenness

of exposure: he's not the only
one. They taught us to say
PINCH ME at a moment of elation,
to ensure we weren't
dreaming, but I have never
said PINCH ME, never blurred

my luck with a good dream, as
I've never dreamt of good things,
only battle cries and cavern
fights and me unarmed and snarled
in my slips, you know I have to
dress this way, I work for tips—

Rondeau with Shouting Attributed to John Connally

MY GOD, THEY'RE GOING TO KILL US ALL,
and I woke from a dream in which I'd died
to find I'm still as dead in life:
no change. I've been to Texas twice;
the second time, my fearful guide—

MY GOD, THEY'RE GOING TO KILL US ALL—
was dressed in crepe. Remember the tape,
the halting car, the governor's
MY GOD, THEY'RE GOING TO KILL US ALL,

as though in end times? Cotton Mather
urged those who would trust one book
to choose Revelation: heaven's last
words before the firing squad,
the smoke and blindfold cinch—MY GOD,
THEY'RE GOING TO KILL US ALL.

Red

Blood that's red

as distinct from blood that's
brown is how you know you need

a doctor now. To read death into
dreams, attend to oceans, avocets,

and F-15s. But what if I dream
of death—what does that mean?

Don't shock the baby into birth
by viewing wretchedness and rape

on-screen, but if you must, repeat
what the suave director

said on the matter of violence
in his movies: THAT'S NOT

BLOOD, THAT'S RED—

PART 2

Teacup This

To my young daughter, I sing the songs

my mother sang to me. Which is to say: to my young daughter,
I sing an eclectic selection of breakup tunes of the '60s and '70s. *Now I know
you're not the only starfish in the sea / If I never hear your name again,
it's all the same to me...* That doesn't seem quite right

to sing to a baby, yet here I am. And here she is: bed-sprawled, unblessed,
and so perhaps like the starfish, yes—one creature of more

than the world requires, as I am unceasingly reminded
by pamphlet mandates, blanket labels, alerts to lay her always up. It's
awful, to be a person. That's why, from my lovers, I've always demanded

to know what kind of a dog I might be, were I ever a dog, and don't
say teacup this, toy that, don't pick a dog that must travel all over stuffed
in a bag like a filthy magazine. Don't take it lightly
when I say of all the men I've been with, there are only a few

I never would allow to hold my child. I consider
this a triumph.

Hot Streak

Actually it's ridiculous to opine on what kind
of a dog I would be, were I ever a dog, as I don't
contain within me half enough life to power
a dog. I WOULD BE A DEAD DOG, THAT'S
WHAT KIND, or maybe a mere industrial object
boasting a low-grade animation, some odd beep
or flicker, like a dryer or a bulb. So, sure, I could
be a reluctant bulb, the only one still offering light
in an otherwise burnt-out fixture bolted
hard to a row house porch. And all those moths,
with no other place to die. Can't they murder
themselves on someone else? Can't they absent
their numbers to the Great North, where there's
only dark, live out their weeks untempted by
glare, die when they're made to, trouble no orb?

All Night to Be Bought Out

I will not speak of my lover except
to say he has requested I stop
asking if he would stay with me,
should I ever be suddenly changed
into a dog. It is not so much that
I want to change, though if I did
wish to dispense with my given form,
would that be so strange? Think of
the weathered men in the breadbasket,
all those rafters, all that heathered
corn. When the Union Pacific came
out to lay track, offering cash
and a ticket south, they waited
in line all night to be bought out.

Home Scale

This decomposing urn,
the ad assures, will turn you, when
you die, into a tree.

Might as well just turn into a tree while you're living.

And what are they
doing, the hospital, asking again
about any self-

harm and then packing the baby into your arms,

saying avoid the dismal
and also remember it's normal
for the baby to lose weight

in the first days, then regain it, you can check by stepping

onto a home scale holding
the baby, then you just subtract
your body from the scene.

Survive Me

It wasn't for love of having

children that I had a child.
Rather, I simply didn't know how a person

could cross, fully shoeless, a bed of coals
and not burn, and I needed

someone to pass this to.
I needed my obtuseness to survive me.

But I never accounted for our thwarting era.
Every day, the paper

runs a remembrance
of a child, the notice struggling to sing the few

years lived: *He never sketched the earth without
its hatch of latitudes. She did*

not like to try new foods.

Were You Lying Then or Are You Lying Now

To be, he said, an American, is to find you have lived
your whole small life on the back of some
starving and saber-toothed creature that has,
all the while, been killing and killing and killing.

No wonder we do so much drinking.

H.'s father went too soon, a suicide.
BETTER TO ASK FORGIVENESS THAN PERMISSION.

Of her partner, Elizabeth Bishop wrote
I DON'T THINK SHE HAD CONSCIOUSLY
PLANNED THIS BECAUSE SHE BROUGHT SO MANY
THINGS—12 KILO BAGS OF COFFEE, ETC.

I remember taking a shot at conversing in Spanish.
When someone mentioned a candidate
for high office, I began to tell the story of going
to see him, in an uncovered field on a hot day

in crucial Ohio. It was noon,

security lines ran long, and people got sick
from the sun and had to sit down. But I didn't

know how to say *sick* or *sit down*, so I just said
everyone died. That's just like death, to creep in
wherever it can, to huddle in wait
in the dooryard of every story. Death is the best

of the lurkers. Death is the worst

sort of lurker, the best sort of soldier of fortune.
It hardly ever refuses anyone's offer.

Was This the Face

Actual children, there are in this world, believing
a burnt plant can be brought back

by spraying under its leaves a green perfume.

Machines can read the date off a dime from orbit.
Flytraps recite IF THIS, THEN THAT. Weather

is thought to be the dead. Of the sun shower,

some say THAT IS MY FATHER. When I die,
they'll point to the toxins blocking the constellations,

say THAT'S YOU. My old love measured his women

in milli-Helens, the unit of female beauty
required to launch only a single ship.

I love that joke involving the Jewish biddies

(THE FOOD IS LOUSY HERE, AND SUCH
SMALL PORTIONS), but I make it instead about God:

God is abusive toward all His children,

and also He hardly ever comes around! If this,
then that. If no news is good news,

then it seems there is no
no news.

The Easy Part Was Hard

I shy from the chore of dying, knowing God
will sort us into separate heavens. I don't
want to be divided. And yes, I understand
it is too much to ask, that heaven be free
of that old impulse to cordon off empires,
mark down who goes where. Still, each next
glimpse of heaven convinces me more
against it. In heaven they still have murder,
but say it's better, because the murder is quickly
solved. Scuba death a little too convenient?
They check the dive computer, have him
cornered in an instant. No need, they boast,
to canvas the city with questions. Still, I have
some questions. When I was a child, I believed
if I lost my key, some evil person would find it
and venture inside. I had no sense of how
he'd have to go home to home forever, suffer
a thousand ill fits in a thousand locks.
It wouldn't be worth the trial, I now know,
living, as I do, so close to heaven. I sleep
against it and wake with its imprint on me.
I remember all the times I nearly died: careening
across Route 3 in the ice or held up with a knife
or seized by an undertow or by his hand.

No Radio

It's true, I wholly missed New York in the '80s.
So you wouldn't remember the cars, he said,

with the dashboard signs NO RADIO, aimed at
deterring thieves from breaking
the windows. O if you love me at all, God, mark

a sign like that on my own self, NOTHING
HERE OF WORTH—I'm tired of having it

come as a surprise. Dutifully I have steeled
to be slighted, and have I been slighted? I have.
Just once I want to hold my child
without considering Europe at the war's end,

the women given armfuls of bluebells
to scatter from their windows, but five years
beating carpets strengthened their arms too much

for the task, and the violet bundles sprayed
on the city like yet another attack.

Beauty School

1.

In the wraparound glass of the beauty
school, a student twists

and pins the hair of a dummy head
up into a nice chignon. *Even the lifeless*

have their indulgences,
I said as I watched an untenable

person eat a whole fish melt
in a single shove. I remembered him bragging

how ugly he was and how keenly
he hated his face, how he avoided

its gaze in restroom mirrors and turned
away when he knelt to the black-front

oven. I am sorry

2.

to bring up Hitler, but you know
what people sometimes say about Hitler—

he was rejected from art school
not on account of any portent

of horrors, but simply because he couldn't
paint realistic-looking faces, only

things. And was this because
he was closed to human fullness. And how

could we try to explain anything
this way. I had worried

3.

I wouldn't be able to pick out the baby
from a crowd, but really

I never encounter a whole crowd
of babies. They exist mostly alone, looking

off, trundled up in a basket or expertly
folded into the dark-

checked sling or slung down
a driven well into which some mother

sings and soothes and hollers
for hours as ropes descend around her.

Passing and Violence

What pride I feel in America stems from our anthem
being the toughest one to sing. The high segment
with the red burn of the rocket: only a few
can reach. Watching a stranger parallel park, I pray
she abrades her neighbor. Watching football, I need
to see a man die. I need to see the intractable passing

and violence. Of the cruelty ringing the earth,
I am a portion. I never said he was *a bad man,* only
a larger portion. He wreaked harm on us for years
and then one day he began to die. I watched as science
shattered his body to wrest the disease out, stopping
just short of his failure. *Failure,* the word
he favored over death. Me, I favored nothing over
death. I held him like a brother. I knew him as an error
of God, dropped at the doorstep of our age, and what
could we do but save him? I began to suspect so many
of machinations. How my parents had summoned me
into this world, but then when I arrived,

they were not here. My whole being was a setup.
They called me over to sit alone with the weather
and soot, unfettered. They said I had differences to be
resolved. After attempting the anthem, upward of fifty
percent remark, *I should have started lower* or *I should
have chosen something else instead.* Uneasy lies the head.

You'd Better Run

Prone was never the way
I pictured Isaac, proving
yet again: of altars, I am all
but ignorant. Of course
he was tied with the soft
side up, simpler to cut
with that which makes
us human. Take this bird
outside of the luncheonette,
the one with the kettle-
fried chip in her beak.
She's unable to break it
small enough to eat, and so
is blessed in her own way,
lacking the nerve or
know-how to hunt what's
hard. Me, I favor gruffness.
I like military haircuts.
I like the inscrutability of
sandbars and of box bombs,
of Bob Dylan, quoting God
when God says kill me
a son. Me, I am always
grappling against the press
of my back to the earth,
but prone was never
the way I pictured Isaac,
because prone just isn't how
it's done: gallows or stake,
when we die for faith,
we stand. Although, come
to think of it, Isaac wasn't

slated for martyrdom;
senseless is the word
I'm searching for.

God Only

The wisdom is this:
when bitten by a cobra,
pray to the skies

the cobra is full-grown.
Adults will ration
their stores of poison,

spit just enough
to stun, while the young
ones, uncontrolled,

give all they've got.
It's supposed to be
the child who

rages and wavers.
It's supposed to be
the child who clumsily

kills. I remember
my old love holding me
once over the side

of some canyon.
DROP ME, I ordered, and
he goddamn tried.

That's right—it is not
God only I have asked
to take my life.

For Later

It took a box of crullers, handed from person to person around
the workroom, to make me understand I can't feel joy. I don't
want sugar on my fingers. Increasingly, I barely experience eating.
It feels as though I am taking a meal and placing it in a coat
pocket. I heard about the rank and murderous city where
the nuns convened to sneak away the infants slated for offing.
They trained a Saint Bernard to bark whenever a little one cried,
to mask the sound. At my side, I keep an adopted blankness,
oafish as a search dog, ever reliable in its great drowning out
of pain. Nobody has to break the news to me that in these waking

years, we each live only a fraction of what's within us. Nobody
has to ask me what my unlived self is doing with its seasons.
It roams the world envisioning all day being killed
like a sow on the slaughter floor, indignant at the artless
worker wiping his hands on his coveralls instead of on a towel.
It boards hot-air balloons, is careless with
the central flame, imagines itself unable to brake and careening
proudly toward the Red Sea, as it has heard that people are
forever recollected and defined by the rooms in which we die,
reduced to the rooms in which we die, and it does not wish to end up

recollected or defined. It does not wish to be reduced, insists
the Red Sea is not a room, and so it has found a way around the way
in which we die. If only I could live that part and not this one.
If only I could shy from the new world's tortured ostentations,
not know candy wheels and concrete, tomes by resolute declinists,
same old *he said, no one else said,* same stooge on the doorstep
unrepentant, having thrashed his path through the world and
pronounced it happenstance, how we are trapped in our bodies
just as, in Dante, the Heathens are trapped in Hell, having
been born in a time of no savior and so not standing a chance.

53

Outside Less

I have been outside less, I have taken to saying,
in the days since my daughter was born—
passive, as though it were somebody

else who bore her. And *bore her,* I also have
taken to saying, as though she were a hole.

I have witnessed a woodpecker force,

through the week, a gape in my neighbor's
barn side. I have watched as my daughter
knocks, woodpecker-like, her searching mouth

into my breast. But I don't mean to say she
instills in my body an absence. What nothing

assembles within me was already there.

Duplex

So much fawning over Lindbergh, why?
Why was it so heralded to fly solo, why is any feat
so drastically diminished by the presence of
a second coursing bloodstream, second blur
of facial features? History adores a lonesome
cabin. And so I accept that I'll never be
remembered; I live in a duplex. And the men
on the southern side of the wall—Dominic
and the other guy—they are the ones who know me.
They are the ones who hear my shrill beseeching
in the halting dawn while they laze around delaying
scraping ice from their side mirrors. They know
I'm this close to giving them the whole house
to themselves. Curled in on myself, I wait
for them to save me. I don't know what they'll
do, but they'll think of something. Each person
on this earth was loved at some point.
Untended infants wither down to nothing,
so when I see an adult or older child,
I am certain that person was at some point loved.
Even the detective on the cop show, with her
swoop of hair and creeping arc about being
conceived in rape. When that character was a baby,
someone nursed her. Someone rocked her, paced
and keened and dimmed the lights as though
in a state of grieving. I saw the episode in which
a man reported hearing a woman screaming
STOP and DON'T from the next apartment.
The twist was that the woman had been bellowing
DON'T STOP DON'T STOP DON'T STOP
at her assailant. She wanted to die.

Can't Go Anywhere

Can't go anywhere these days
without being told a turtle
has nerve endings in its shell.
Brush up against it, it feels you.
Scratch on it like a murderer
on top of an urban legend
car, knowing just how to get
the lovers' attention,

it feels you. Once, I tried
to acquire a noise machine.
It wasn't for hatred of silence,
but to dampen a different
noise I couldn't stand to hear.
The store had RAIN, it had TIN
ROOF RAIN, it had RAIN HEARD
FROM THE INSIDE OF A CAR.
If there'd been one for NAILS
OF A KILLER, I would've

shelled out. Once, I attended
a dance show where the dancers
played at having one life
between them. Each took a turn
at flailing and then barreled
into the next one and went ashen.
I wanted to go up there. I'd give
myself to anyone, if I could.

Reformation Window

Nothing against false houses. It's just maintaining
a bird feeder too much reminds me of how
I typically live: not only unseen by those I admire,
but thoroughly unimagined. And the holes they boast
instead of doors, like a bank vault entered by blasting.
I can't stop thinking of violence done to buildings.
Why isn't there a church with a stained-glass window
extolling the Reformation, the window depicting
only a door, and the congregants queuing up to drive
the 95 Theses through it and shatter the scene?

Six months from now, another election will choke us
where we live. Six months from now, my elsewhere
friends will call to ask, *Ohio, will you carry it, will you deliver,*
as though discussing a child, the child arriving onto
the sudden doctor, onto the scale and form on
which they print the name. Six months from now, an ad
will appear: *Apartment for let, all rooms have closing
doors.* Six months from now, the air will turn
wooly and red with emissions, and then it will clear
and recur, and the world will be older. I'll be dead.

Form, Save for My Own

Even a baby stares
longer at symmetrical
faces, it's said, than

at faces uneven,
suggesting a preference
for pattern, a want

inborn. But what
if the baby is staring
instead in horror?

I revere all variants
of the human
form, save for my own.

My mind has made
an enemy of my body;
it's all I can do

not to quote Kissinger
on the Iran-Iraq
War: A PITY THEY

BOTH CAN'T LOSE.

Mostly Rasputin

Stuck at a party next to the kind of doctor
who also can give pills, I did not fault him.

I've had lovers with others on the mind.
Charged with attention always, who could not drift

to, say, how untried cowboys may find kissing
unduly burdensome, due to the hats?

I have a specific question regarding dosage.

You hear about these people, mostly Rasputin,
imbued with enormity and a psychic block

when it comes to submitting to death. There's never
a sufficiently tireless clubbing, never enough

cyanide in the wine. If I had to guess, I doubt
I'll have that problem.

Low Blow

Death like a word I heard once and then
everywhere. And still the dart-bar town
was lousy with life: the high school band
that had to learn the march before the music

and spread across the tar in silent shapes.
And the heat, with its uncertain grip,
like a child's hand required to always be held
when crossing streets. And the heat, like

an insult that stayed with me all day. And
the heat, like red paint thrown on me
in protest, I didn't know why. And the heat,
like another animal's skin I wear as a disguise.

Ten What

The camera adds ten what, I can't remember.
But the threat's enough to make me stay

away. I don't want any more of what I have.
I don't want another spider plant. I don't

want another lover. Especially I don't want
another clock, except insofar as each of us

is a clock, all hammers and counting
down. And yes, I know by heart the list

of lifetimes. A worker bee will die before
a camel. A fox will die before a pilot whale.

A pocket watch will die before the clock inside
the crocodile—I think of this often, but never

tell my lover, as I do not tell him that,
upstairs, a moth is pinned by the window

sash. I make no plans to free it. Everyone says
the baby looks like me, but I can't see it.

The Sky

Whatever I care for, someone else loves it
more, deserves it more: the doe with her
whole mouth crushing the phlox or the seer
who adores my future, whereas I could

take it or leave it. I know I'll disappear.
It won't be glamorous. It won't be like when
the *Mona Lisa* was stolen and the tourists all
lined up to pay their respects at the empty
spot on the wall of the Louvre.

I've never actually even seen the sky.
I've only ever seen effluents, seen wattage.

The only night I remember is the dinner
of neighbors at which a man I never
had met before said *I don't fear dying*—

look at the past, people have been dying forever, and—

then he stopped and shook his head—
*I drank too much. I was almost saying
that people have died forever and all
of them survived, but of course*—he made
a hard laugh—*God, of course they didn't survive.*

I am immensely grateful to many people who have helped this book along with their smarts and kindness. Thank you, in particular, to Meg Shevenock, Jamie Boyle, Cormac Slevin, Tyler Meier, David Baker, Sergei Lobanov-Rostovsky, Jennifer Clarvoe, Henry Israeli, Sarah Blake, Rebecca Lauren Gidjunis, Colin Walker, Becky Alexander, Sorelle Friedler, Elizabeth Lindsey Rogers, Jesse Quillian, Ida Stewart, Elisabeth Breese, Letitia Trent, Adam Clay, Greg Williamson, and Megan Peak. Thank you to Michael Wiegers, Elaina Ellis, Kelly Forsythe, Tonaya Craft, Emily Grise, and everyone at Copper Canyon Press. Erin Belieu's guidance has been instrumental. Kathy Fagan always knows the answer. Pablo Tanguay is frighteningly insightful. I kept on flailing in the water, and David Lynn kept on pulling me out.

This book was completed with the generous support of a *Kenyon Review* Fellowship, a Literature Fellowship from the National Endowment for the Arts, a Ruth Lilly Fellowship from the Poetry Foundation, and a GLCA New Writers Award. Thank you to my colleagues at Tufts University, Kenyon College, and the *Kenyon Review.*

Thank you also to Adrienne and Brett Stephenson, to Marvin and Shirlee Shapero, to Rick and Diane Crano, to Brendan and Gianna and Steve. And Martha. Thank you to my partner, Ricky, who sustains me every day with his genius and strength. And to our daughter: more than ever, Frankie Now!

About the Author

Natalie Shapero is the Professor of the Practice of Poetry at Tufts University and an editor at large of the *Kenyon Review*. She lives in Somerville, Massachusetts.

Poetry is vital to language and living. Since 1972, Copper Canyon Press has published extraordinary poetry from around the world to engage the imaginations and intellects of readers, writers, booksellers, librarians, teachers, students, and donors.

WE ARE GRATEFUL FOR THE MAJOR SUPPORT PROVIDED BY:

THE PAUL G. ALLEN
FAMILY FOUNDATION

TO LEARN MORE ABOUT UNDERWRITING
COPPER CANYON PRESS TITLES,
PLEASE CALL 360-385-4925 EXT. 103

WE ARE GRATEFUL FOR THE MAJOR SUPPORT PROVIDED BY:

Anonymous

Jill Baker and Jeffrey Bishop

Donna and Matt Bellew

John Branch

Diana Broze

Sarah and Tim Cavanaugh

Janet and Les Cox

Catherine Eaton and David E.
    Skinner

Beroz Ferrell & The Point, LLC

Mimi Gardner Gates

Linda Gerrard and Walter Parsons

Gull Industries, Inc.
    on behalf of William and
    Ruth True

Rose Gummow

Steven Myron Holl

Lakeside Industries, Inc.
    on behalf of Jeanne Marie Lee

Maureen Lee and Mark Busto

Rhoady Lee and Alan Gartenhaus

Ellie Mathews and Carl Youngmann
    as The North Press

Anne O'Donnell and John Phillips

Suzie Rapp and Mark Hamilton

Joseph C. Roberts

Jill and Bill Ruckelshaus

Cynthia Lovelace Sears and
    Frank Buxton

Seattle Foundation

Kim and Jeff Seely

Dan Waggoner

Austin Walters

Barbara and Charles Wright

The dedicated interns and
    faithful volunteers of
    Copper Canyon Press

The Chinese character for poetry is made up of two parts: "word"
and "temple." It also serves as pressmark for
Copper Canyon Press.

The poems are set in Requiem.
Headings are set in Akzidenz Grotesk.
Printed on archival-quality paper.
Book design and composition by Phil Kovacevich.